1. The Army of the Cumberland was given new flags in August 1863. The central design featured the bald eagle found in the Great Seal of the United States. It also incorporated the national colors and a star. Colors: diagonal stripes from top to bottom are red, white, and dark blue; central disk is light blue with a gold star; eagle is dark brown with a white head and a gold beak and legs; olive branch is green; arrowheads are white; central shield is dark blue at the top with red and white stripes below and a gold border; letters are gold.

2. Field artillery companies had special flags, but when they served as infantry or as foot or fortress artillery the flag shown here was displayed. Different colors were associated with different branches of the army—blue with infantry, yellow with artillery, scarlet with engineers, etc. The number of a regiment would be included on the ribbon of the standard model flag (shown here) when an actual banner was made for use. Cords and tassels were attached to the flagpole which had a spearhead at the top. Colors: field is yellow; ribbons are red with gold borders & lettering; crossed cannon are bronze.

3. The regimental "color" (flag) for infantry has always been blue. The central design is the eagle taken from the Great Seal. The stars were originally silver but at the time of the Civil War were usually painted in gold. The number of the regiment was included on the ribbon below the eagle. Colors: field is dark blue; eagle is brown with a white head and tail and gold beak and feet; laurel branch is green; arrows and stars are gold; ribbons are red with gold borders and inscriptions.

3. INFANTRY REGIMENT

1. RESERVE CORPS HEADQUARTERS FLAG

2. ARTILLERY REGIMENT

CONFEDERAT

NAVAL JAC

Today everyc recognizes this sign as the "Cc federate Bat Flag," but at t time of the Ci War it was actua used as a jack Confederate na vessels. The jack flown on the pr of a ship. Togeth with the ensig flown at the ste it identifies t nationality o vessel. Colors: t field is red; the d gonal cross is da blue with wh borders; the st are white.

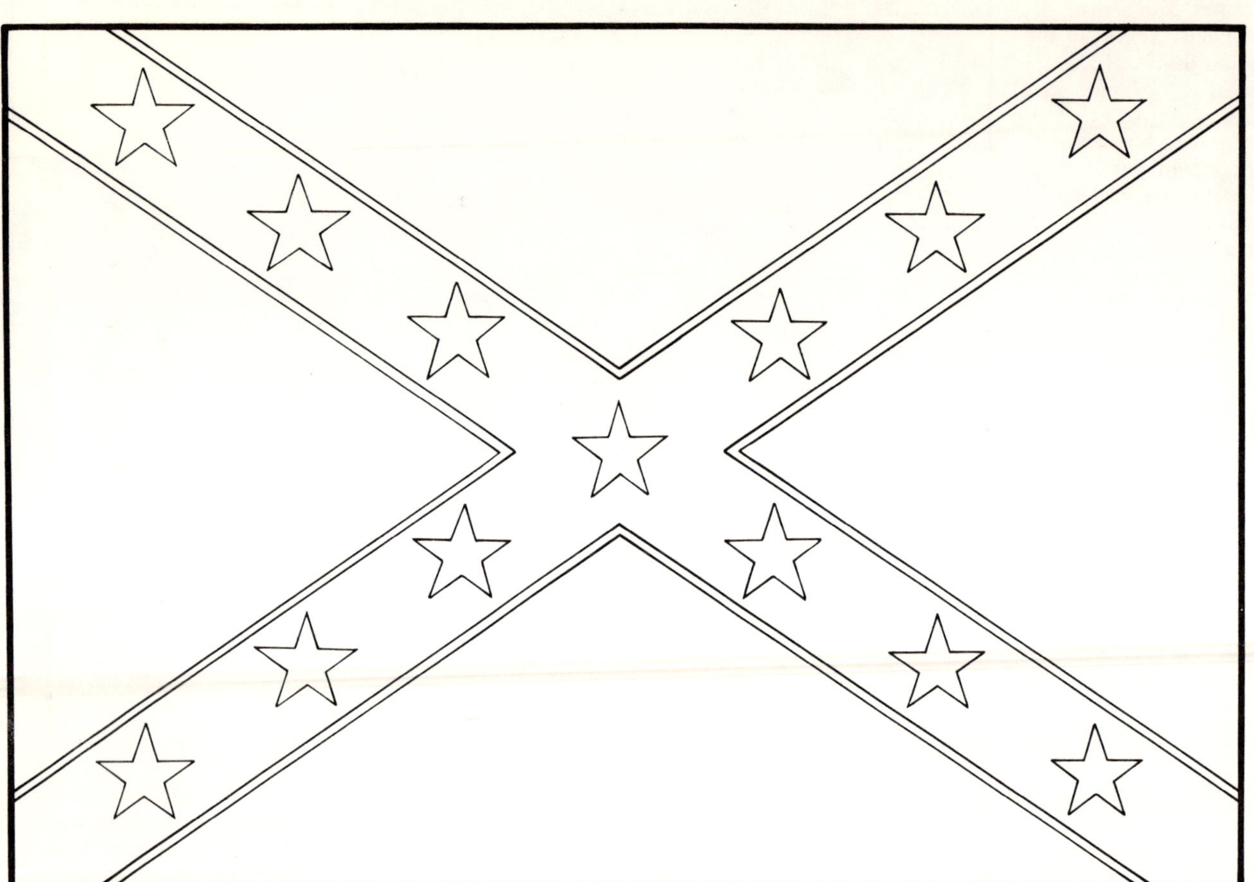

NORTH

CAROLINA

It is remarkable how many flags in American history have been patterned after the Stars and Stripes. Even though it had seceded from the Union, North Carolina in 1861 turned to that flag as an inspiration for its own. The three colors, the two stripes and star were all borrowed from the national flag. The dates are for the Mecklenburg Declaration of Independence (which North Carolina supposedly adopted in 1775) and for the secession of 1861. Colors: white letters on red; blue top stripe, white bottom stripe.

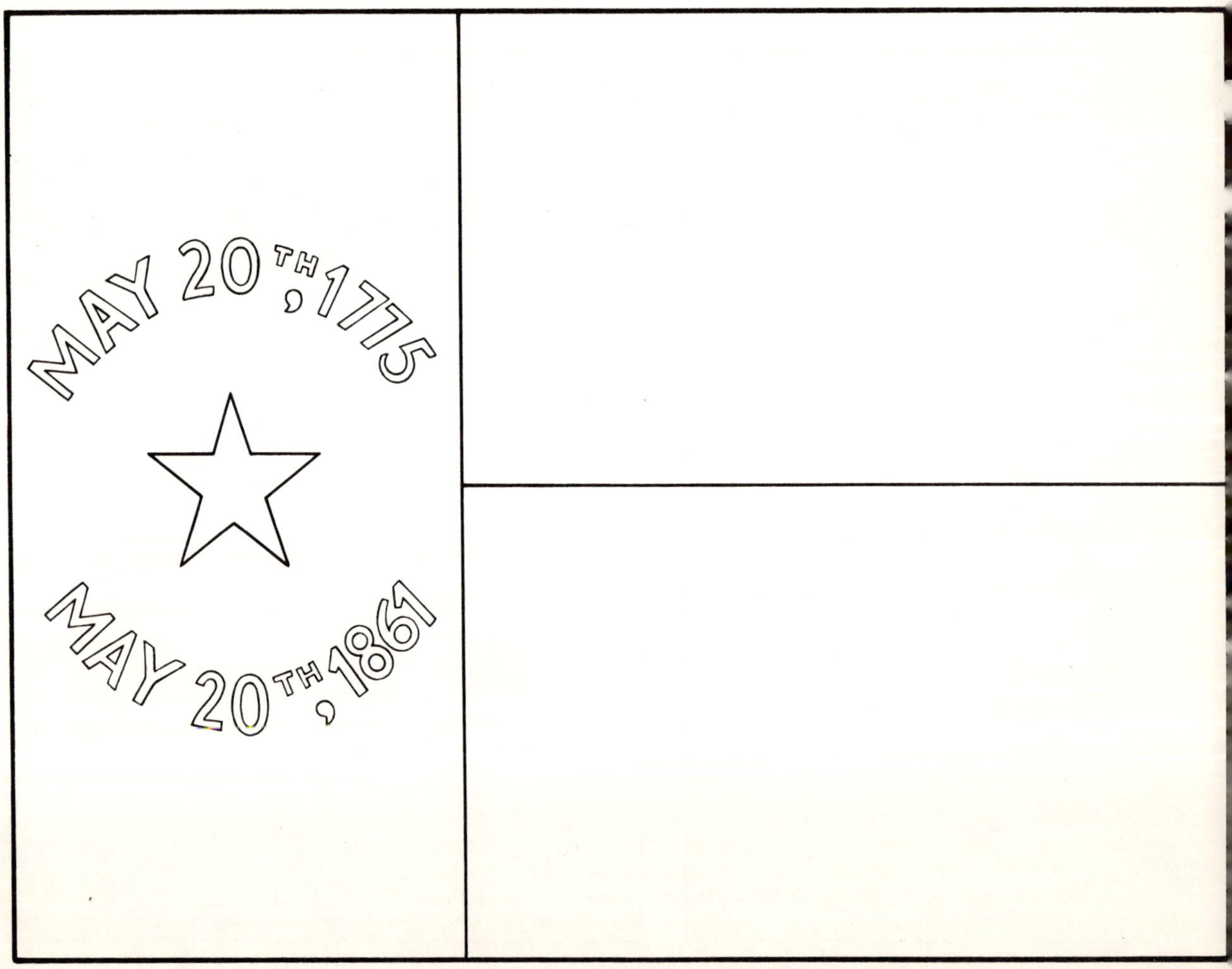

GENERAL GRANT'S HEADQUARTERS Ulysses S. Grant chose the simple Stars and Stripes as the flag to mark his headquarters. It had 36 stars although officially the 36th star (for Nevada) was not added until the Fourth of July 1865, after the end of the Civil War. Rows of stars were only one of many patterns in that era. They became more common in the late 19th century as the number of stars increased. While the stars stand for states, no particular state can claim an individual star. Also, the thirteen stripes stand collectively for the thirteen original states; no one stripe stands for a particular state. Colors: the canton is light blue with white stars; there are seven red and six white stripes.

GENERAL BURNSIDE'S COMMAND HEADQUARTERS The purpose of flags is to identify and inspire. During the Civil War thousands of different flags were used by military units, individuals, government institutions, and private citizens. Before it became part of the Army of the Potomac, the command under General Ambrose Burnside used this distinctive flag. It was based on the national flag but with a cannon and anchor to symbolize artillery and naval operations. The flagstaff was a pike of the kind used in the 18th century to help marching soldiers keep in formation. The flag was attached to it by rings passing through metal grommets in the flag. Other flags had a sleeve that slipped over the pole or were attached to the staff by ribbons or halyards (ropes). Colors: there are seven red and six white stripes; the canton is light blue with white stars; the shield is white with a gold cannon and red anchor.

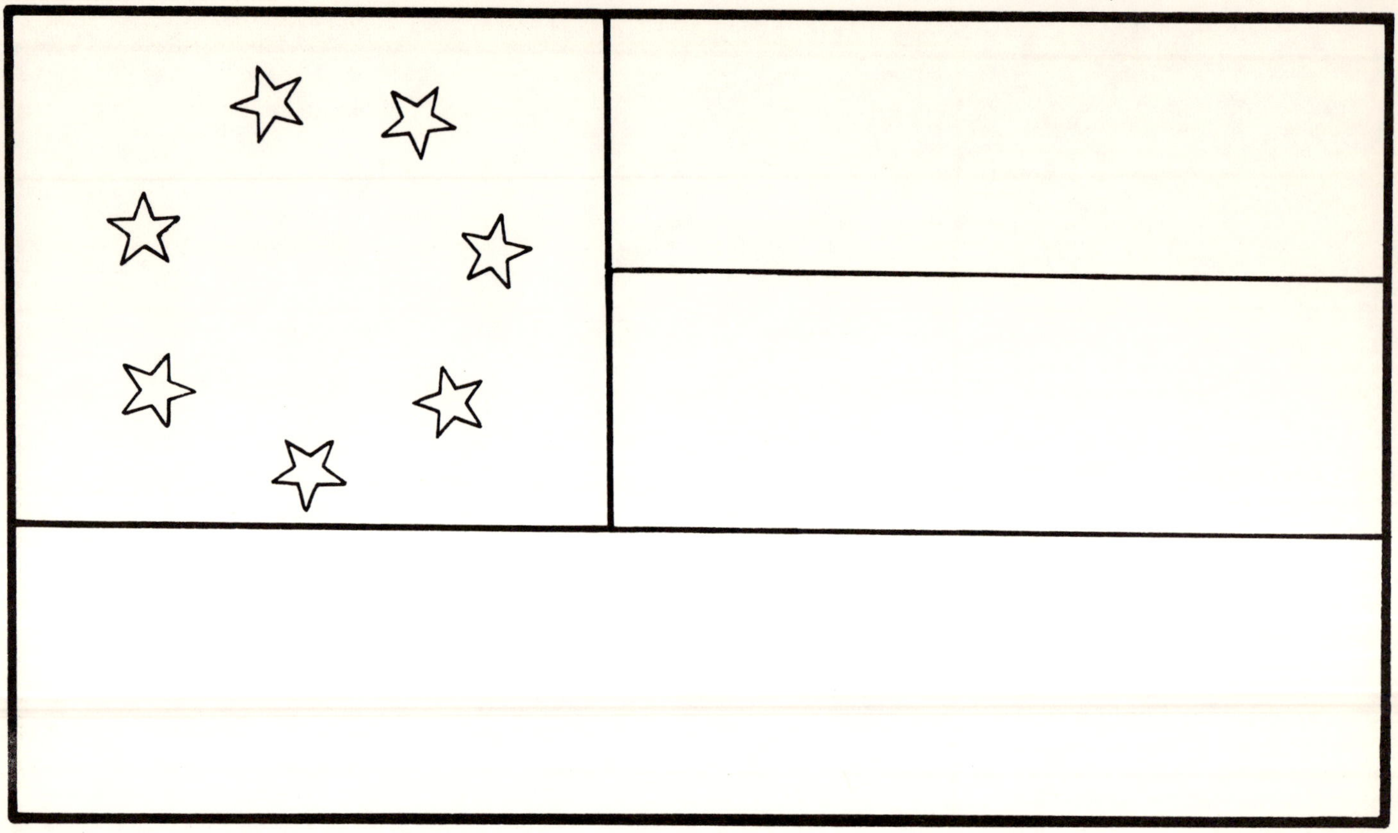

STARS AND BARS The Confederate States of America was organized in Montgomery, Alabama, in February 1861. Many people sent proposals for flag designs, including Nicola Marschall. His design was chosen in March as the national flag, although never officially recognized by the Confederate Congress. It strongly resembles the Stars and Stripes, although some have pointed out that it is similar to the Austrian national flag (horizontal red-white-red stripes) under which Marschall served before emigrating to the United States. The stars were supposed to represent the states in the Confederacy. Originally seven in number, they increased to fifteen. Kentucky and Missouri each had two governments, one loyal to the North and one to the South. Many Confederate flags therefore show only thirteen stars. Colors: the horizontal stripes are red, white, and red; the canton is dark blue with white stars.

MISSISSIPPI FLAG A comedian named Harry McCarthy wrote and sang "The Bonnie Blue Flag," which became very popular in the South in the early days of the Civil War. It was inspired by the flag that had been hoisted over the state capitol of Mississippi on 9 January 1861 when the state seceded from the Union. The same month the flag shown here was adopted for the "independent republic of Mississippi". Painted in the middle was a large magnolia tree, recognized since 1938 as the official state tree of Mississippi. In the mid-19th century most American states did not have flags of their own. Those adopted later in the century were largely based on Civil War era designs, both in the North and the South. Colors: the field is white; the canton is blue with a white star; the vertical stripe at the fly is red; the magnolia tree is brown with green leaves and white flowers.

12th REGIMENT OF INFANTRY

The national color, carried into battle by a color-bearer, was an impressive sight. Six foot square in size on a nine-foot pole, it could be seen for great distances and was an inspiration to the soldiers. These flags were made of silk and today those which survive are usually in poor condition. (The silk, when being prepared, was washed in metal salts that eventually rotted the fibers.) The stars in these flags were frequently of gold rather than white, possibly because of the emblems of rank worn by officers. Later a "gold star mother" was one whose son had died in battle. The arrangement of the stars was not specified and many variations existed. The present, standardized form of the national flag was adopted in 1912 by President William Howard Taft with later modification under Presidents Wilson and Eisenhower. The inscription on this flag means the 12th Regiment of Infantry, Corps d'Afrique. This was the (French) name given to black troops at the beginning of the war. Colors: the canton is dark blue with stars of gold; the fringe is gold; there are seven red and six white stripes; the inscription is gold.

5th REGIMENT

U.S. HEAVY ARTILLERY

Company C of the regiment received a splendid banner "presented by the colored citizens of Natchez, Mississippi." As was usual in those days, the design was painted in oil; every flag was unique and each was a work of art. Black Americans participated extensively, especially in the Union Army, throughout the Civil War. Colors: field is yellow; the ribbons are red with gold inscriptions and borders; the other emblems are gold.

STAINLESS BANNER After two years of war, many Southerners felt it was inappropriate to fly a flag (the Stars and Bars) so close in design to the Stars and Stripes. In May 1863, therefore, a new flag was adopted. The "Battle Flag" then being introduced in the armies of the South was established as the canton on a plain white flag. Because General Stonewall Jackson had his coffin covered with this flag soon after its adoption, it was often known as the "Jackson Flag." It was also called the "Stainless Banner." Its similarity to a flag of truce led to a change in the design in the last days of the war. Colors: white field; red canton; dark blue saltire; white borders and stars.

APPOMATTOX FLAG This was the official Confederate national flag when Lee surrendered at Appomattox Courthouse. The proportions were shortened and a red vertical stripe was added at the fly end. It had been approved by the Confederate Congress on 4 March 1865. Colors: white field with a vertical red stripe at the fly end; red canton; dark blue saltire with white borders; white stars.

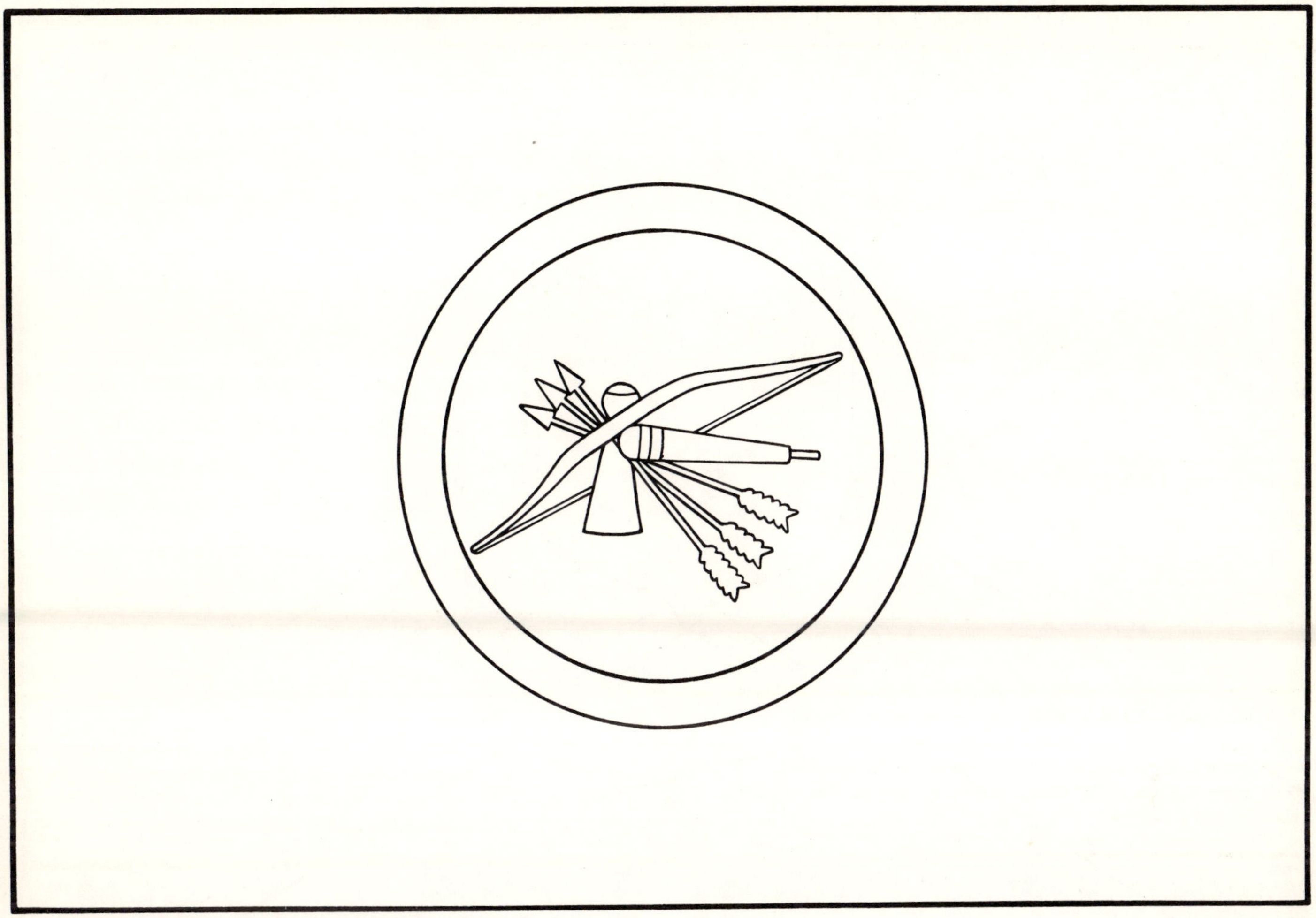

CHOCTAW FLAG

A troop of Choctaw soldiers served in the Confederate army. Their flag contained the emblem used by the tribe. The bow is not strung, indicating that the Choctaw were a peaceful people, but always ready to defend themselves. Colors: blue background; red central disk with a white border; white peacepipe, bow, and arrows.

ARMY OF THE WEST

Major General Van Dorn set the pattern for a Confederate battle flag used in Texas, Mississippi, Arkansas, and Missouri. This one was carried by the 40th Mississippi Volunteers. The crescent was a symbol of the South in New Orleans and South Carolina. The stars are for the Confederate states.

Colors: red field; white stars and crescent; yellow border on the three outer edges; white border along the hoist (where the flag is attached to the pole).

FIRST AND THIRD FLORIDA VOLUNTEERS

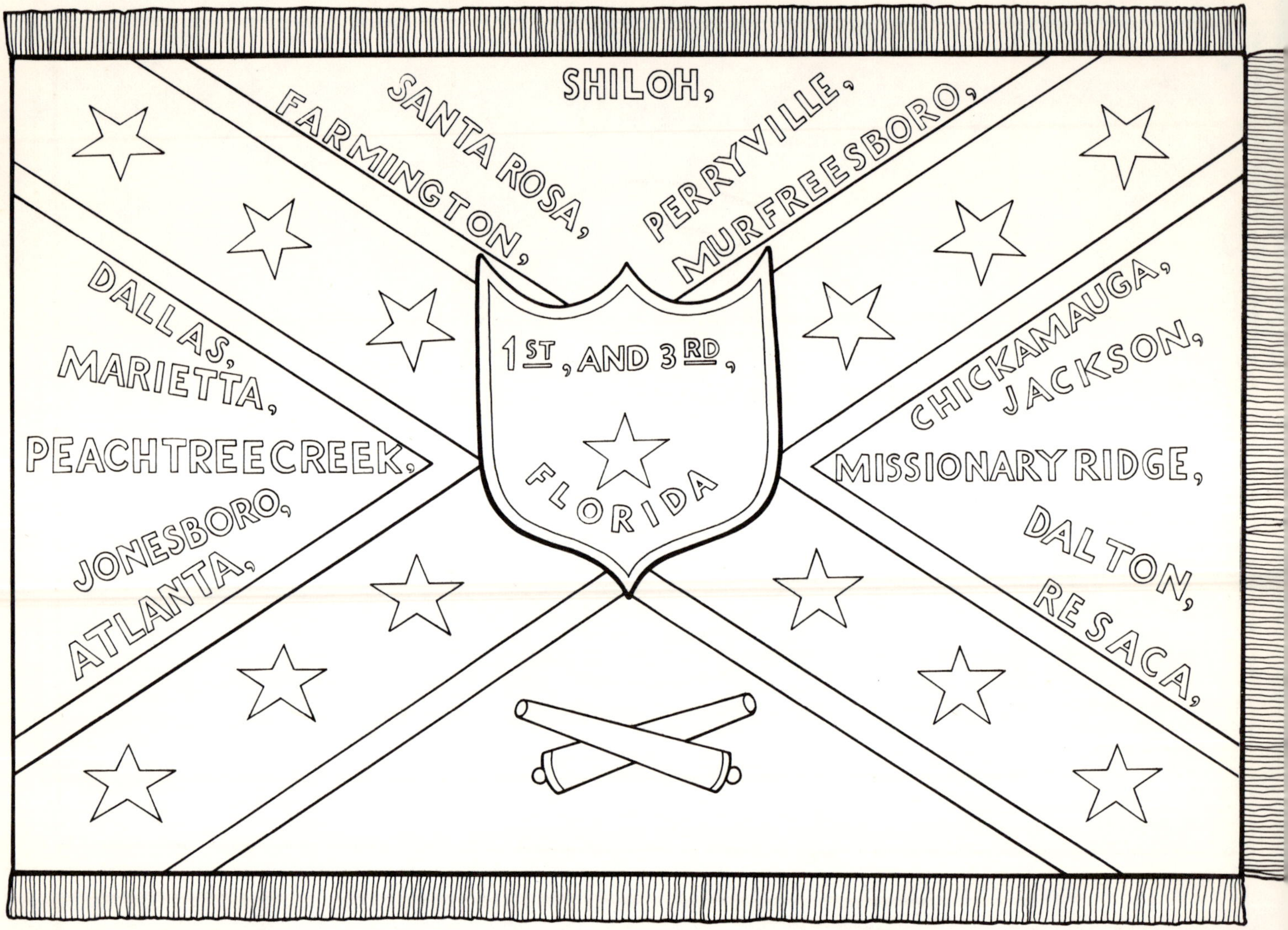

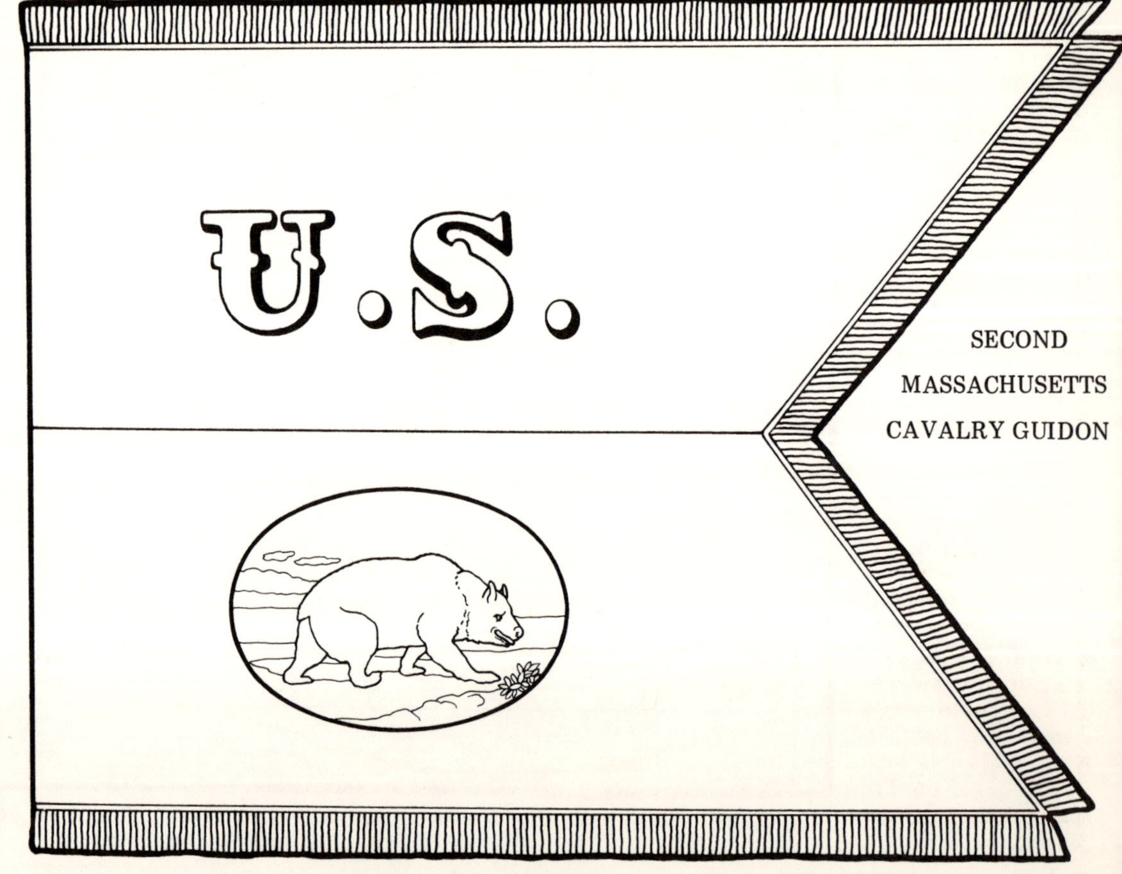

The combined 1st and 3rd Regiments of Florida Volunteers inscribed on its battle flags the names of all the engagements it participated in. The stars on the saltire (diagonal cross) are made of silk reinforced with old sheet music. The original flag is today in the Museum of the Confederacy, Richmond, Virginia. Colors: red background; white saltire with dark blue borders; red central shield with a gold border; white star and inscriptions; rose-colored stars on saltire; gold cannon; white fringe.

SECOND MASSACHUSETTS CAVALRY GUIDON

Sentiments of Californians were divided during the Civil War. One group that wanted to fight on behalf of the Union successfully requested recognition as a special unit, the 2nd Massachusetts Cavalry. Their guidon is today in the California State Capitol museum. A guidon was carried by cavalry troops to *guide the men on* so that they could see the direction of their unit in the heat of battle. Colors: red top stripe with gold letters; white bottom stripe; dark brown bear; blue sky; grassy field.

Polk's Corps of Withers' Division (the 10th Mississippi Volunteers) carried this flag in late 1863. Although it has the same colors and general design as the famous Confederate Battle Flag, it is really quite different. The number of stars on Confederate flags varied from nine to thirteen. (Only thirteen states actively participated in the Confederate government.) Here the "Southern Cross" with a star for each state appears in the national colors of the Confederacy. Crossed cannon have been added—probably on the battlefield—to indicate the capture of Union artillery. Battle honors won by the Volunteers also were sewn on in white cotton lettering. Colors: dark blue field; red cross with white borders; white stars, crossed cannon and inscriptions.

Thomas Francis Meagher, an Irish revolutionary in 1848, came to the United States. In 1862 he was appointed to command the Federal Irish Brigade raised in New York as part of the state volunteers. Their first regimental color was lost in the first Battle of Bull Run in July 1861. Under Meagher they received a new regimental color in November of the same general design. It showed the national symbol of Ireland, a harp, surrounded by shamrocks. The sun of liberty is breaking through the clouds above. A motto in Gaelic ("Who Never Retreated From the Clash of Spears") is inscribed below and the name of the unit appears on a ribbon above. Colors: dark green background; gold sun and harp; light green shamrocks; white clouds; red ribbons with gold inscriptions.

69th REGIMENT

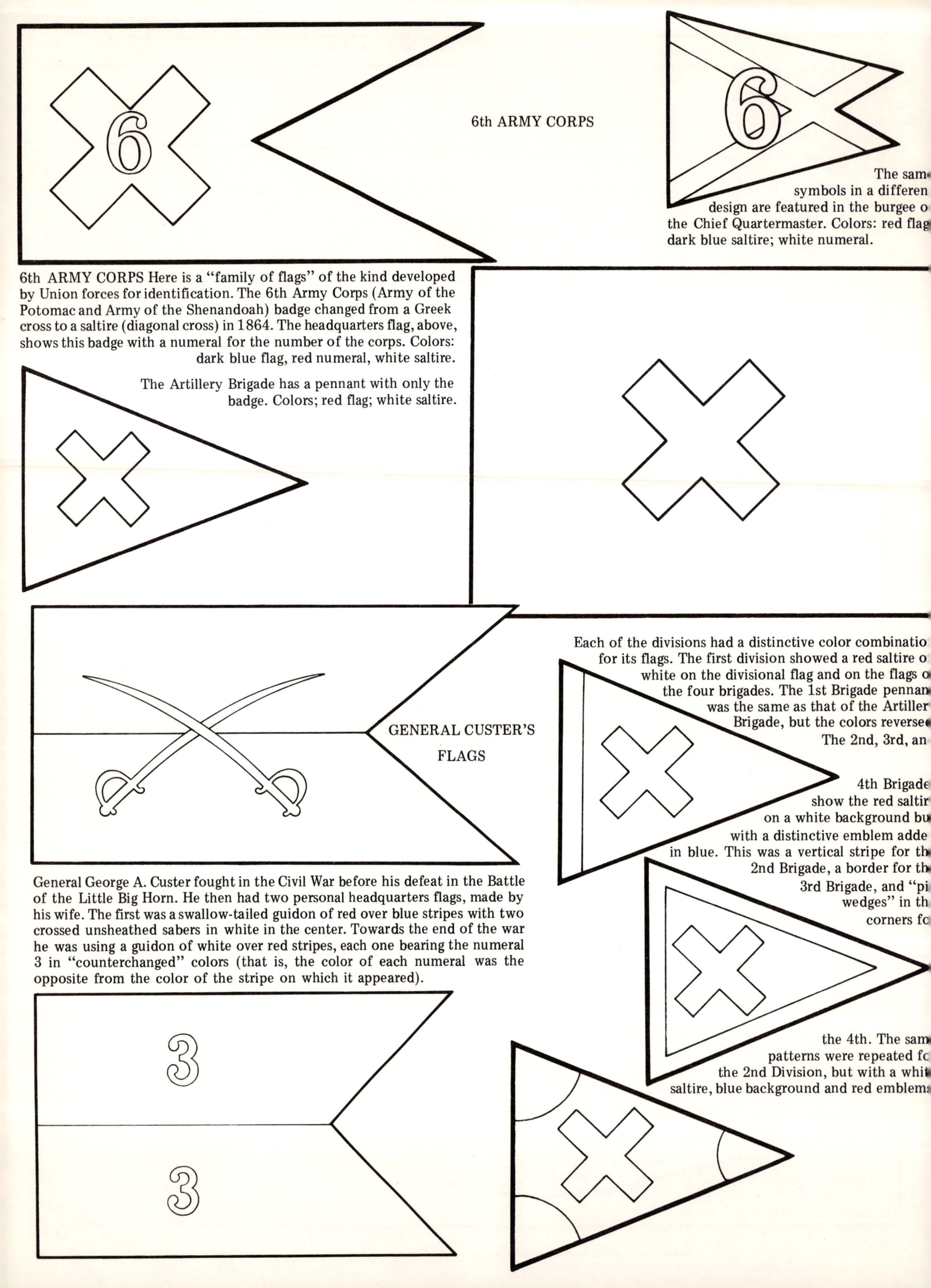

6th ARMY CORPS

The same symbols in a different design are featured in the burgee of the Chief Quartermaster. Colors: red flag, dark blue saltire; white numeral.

6th ARMY CORPS Here is a "family of flags" of the kind developed by Union forces for identification. The 6th Army Corps (Army of the Potomac and Army of the Shenandoah) badge changed from a Greek cross to a saltire (diagonal cross) in 1864. The headquarters flag, above, shows this badge with a numeral for the number of the corps. Colors: dark blue flag, red numeral, white saltire.

The Artillery Brigade has a pennant with only the badge. Colors; red flag; white saltire.

GENERAL CUSTER'S FLAGS

General George A. Custer fought in the Civil War before his defeat in the Battle of the Little Big Horn. He then had two personal headquarters flags, made by his wife. The first was a swallow-tailed guidon of red over blue stripes with two crossed unsheathed sabers in white in the center. Towards the end of the war he was using a guidon of white over red stripes, each one bearing the numeral 3 in "counterchanged" colors (that is, the color of each numeral was the opposite from the color of the stripe on which it appeared).

Each of the divisions had a distinctive color combination for its flags. The first division showed a red saltire on white on the divisional flag and on the flags of the four brigades. The 1st Brigade pennant was the same as that of the Artillery Brigade, but the colors reversed. The 2nd, 3rd, and 4th Brigade show the red saltire on a white background but with a distinctive emblem added in blue. This was a vertical stripe for the 2nd Brigade, a border for the 3rd Brigade, and "pie wedges" in the corners for the 4th. The same patterns were repeated for the 2nd Division, but with a white saltire, blue background and red emblems.

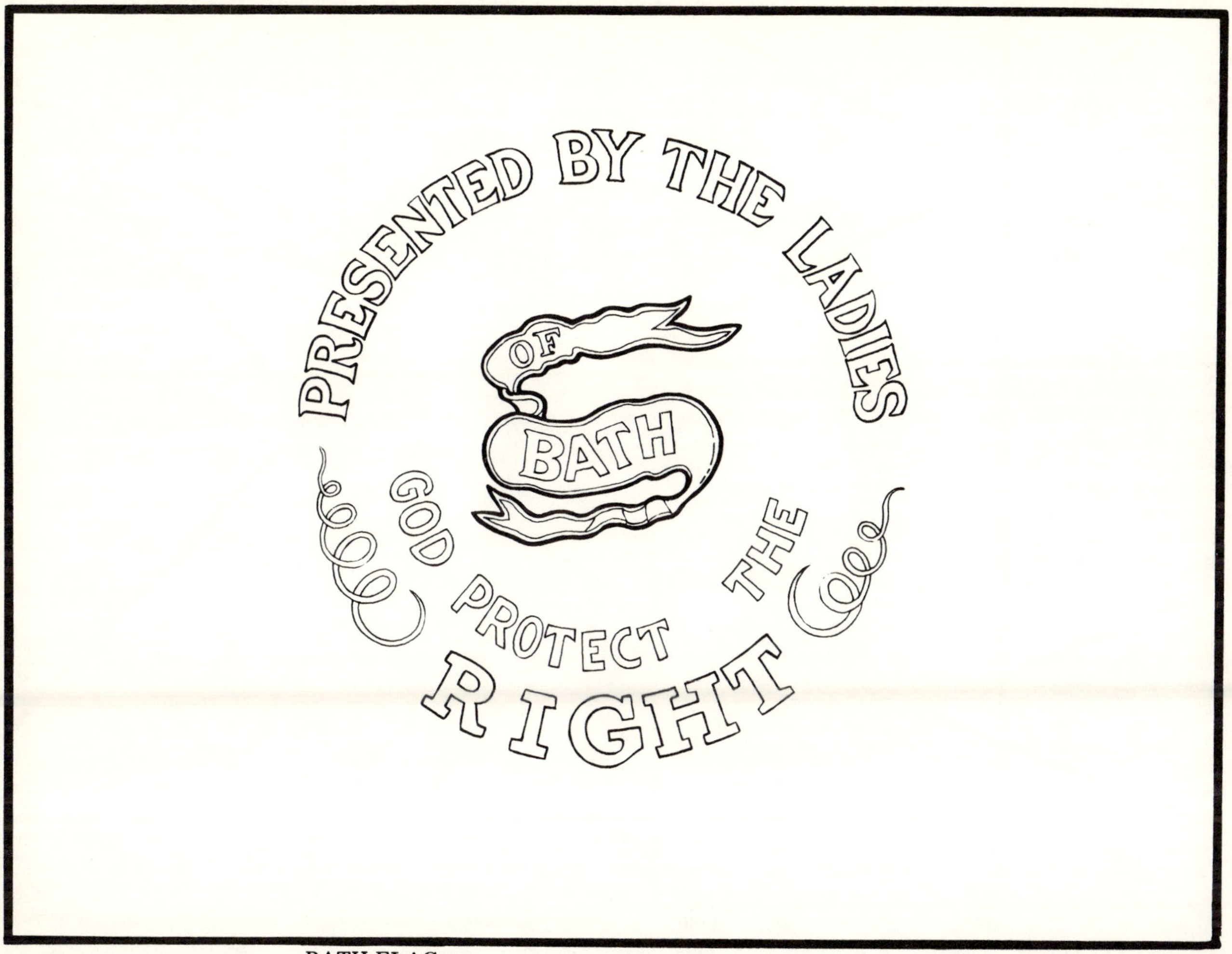

BATH FLAG

A group of women from Bath County, Virginia, made a flag to be carried by troops from that area. The flag, about which nothing else is known, had fringe along the outer edges as decoration. Colors: blue field, white letters and outline of the central ribbon.

Brigadier General W.J. Hardee organized Southern troops which carried as a battle flag a dark blue field with a white border and a white central disk (or oval). The name of the unit carrying the banner was usually inscribed in the center as in this example. It was also common for "battle honors"—that is, the names of battles in which the unit had honorably participated—to be added to the flag. In 1864 Hardee's troops, by then the division of the Army of Tennessee under Major General Cleburne, were ordered to carry the Southern Cross battle flag. The men resisted giving up their old familiar flags and the banner seen here was carried until its capture by Indiana troops. Colors: dark blue field; black central emblems on a white central oval; white border and other inscriptions.

THIRD CONFEDERATE INFANTRY

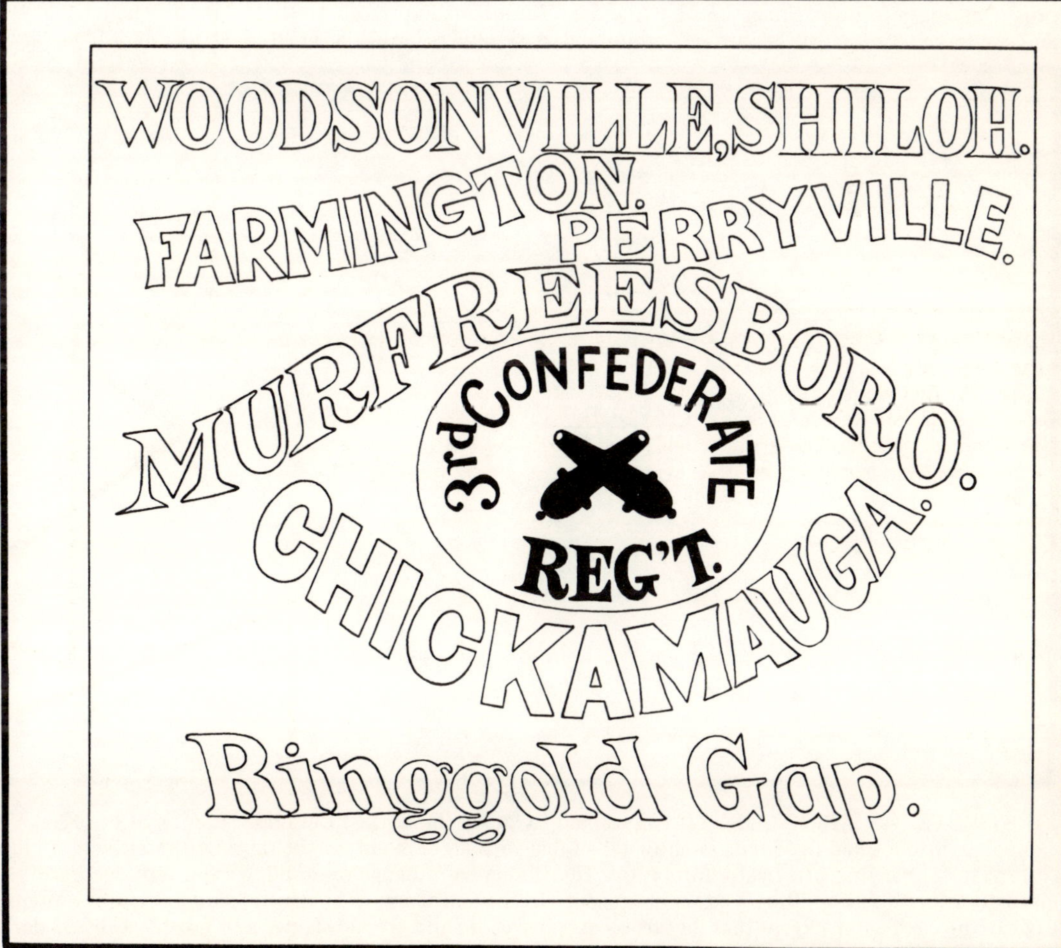

Lance pennons were a tradition introduced into Europe by the Turks and Tatars. The first cavalry troops to make extensive use of them were from Poland and the Polish national colors (red and white) were commonly used by many other countries who adopted the style. It may have been for this reason that the cavalry guidon in the United States was traditionally red over white horizontal stripes. (Lance pennons have never regularly been used by American forces.) This flag was easily confused, however, with the Stars and Bars of the Confederacy. Therefore, in January 1862 a swallow-tailed version of the Stars and Stripes was adopted for use as the Union cavalry guidon. It continued in use until 1885. The guidon shown here was made before the change in design. Colors: the top stripe is red with white lettering; the bottom stripe is white with red lettering.

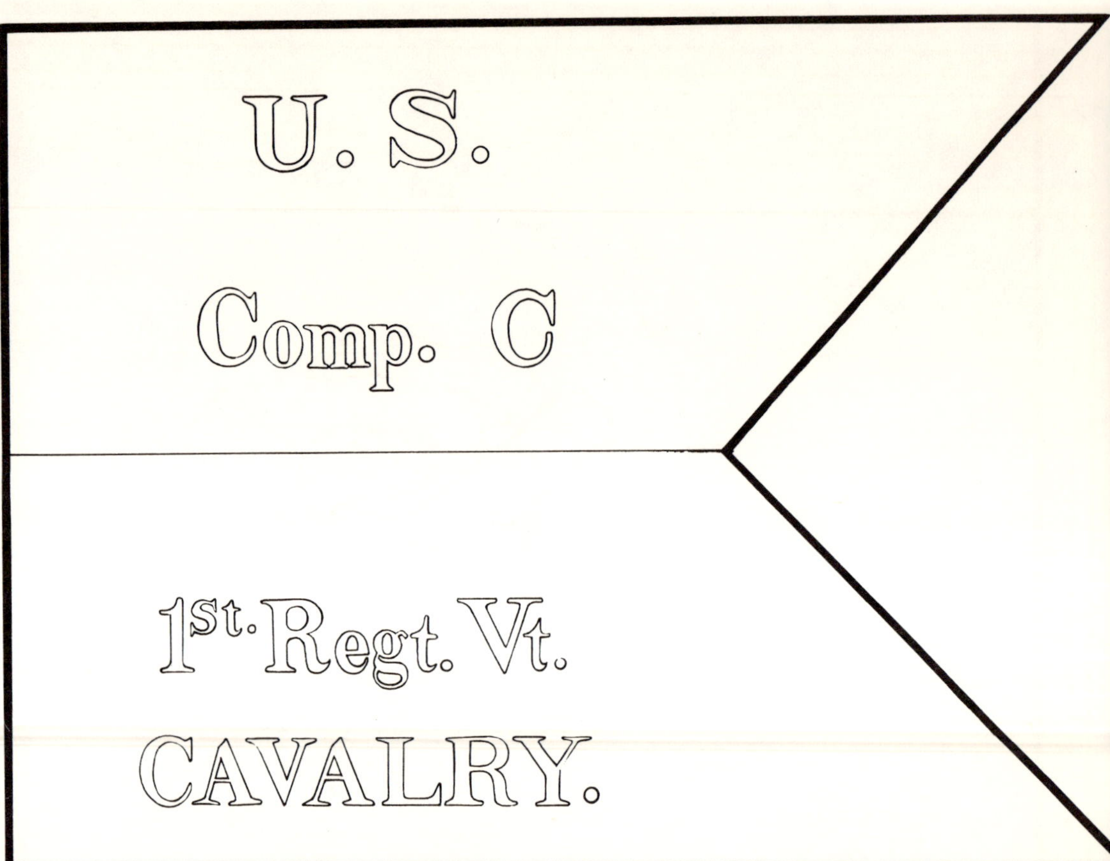

Next page: Today military colors are made under the direction of the Quartermaster General according to detailed specifications. Unofficial flags are not allowed and even the variations in design from regiment to regiment are slight. At the time of the Civil War, in contrast, there were few flag regulations and many were ignored. This flag is an example of the interesting, eccentric designs invented by the men who went to war (or by their ladies). The battle honors and dates comprise practically a history of the whole war. Spaces that would otherwise be empty are filled with flowers, weapons, stars, etc. This "battle flag" was carried by Battery A of the 5th Artillery Regiment. Colors: the field is scarlet; the designs, inscriptions, and fringe are gold.

Next page: Troops from Iowa captured this flag at the Battle of Champion's Hill, also known as Baker's Creek, in 1863. Like many military organizations before and since, the 31st Alabama Volunteers expressed on their flag their belief that their cause was justified by religion and patriotism. Colors: stripes are red, white, red; dark blue inscription on white stripe; dark blue canton with white cross, stars, letters.

FIRST VETERAN ARMY CORPS If you wanted to locate the tent of General Hancock of the First Veteran Army Corps during a field campaign, you looked for a blue swallow-tailed flag with an emblem. In the days before radio communications flags were an important system for conveying practical information. This design has a badge resembling a military decoration with a wreath of leaves like those given to athletic and military victors in ancient Greece and Rome. The central shield resembles the one on the breast of the American eagle in the Great Seal, execpt that the latter has seven white and six red stripes and no star. Colors: dark blue background; green wreath; white central badge; the shield is blue in the middle with white stars above and has seven red and six white stars at the bottom.

RICHMOND

18 61

Drewry's Bluff
Yorktown
Gaine's Mills
Malvern Hill
South Mountain

Cold Harbor
Antietam
Fredericksburg
Suffolk
Ashby's Gap

18 65

Petersburg
Appomattox C.H.
Surrender of ARMY of NORTHERN VIRGINIA

5th ARTILLERY REGIMENT FLAG

GOD AND OUR NATIVE LAND

THIRTYFIRSTALABAMA

31st ALABAMA VOLUNTEERS

CAVALRY GUIDON

Made of silk, the cavalry guidon soon wore out in use and needed to be replaced. The stars were painted in oils and gold was favored. The same gold paint was sometimes used to add battle inscriptions to the stripes of the flag. There is no special significance to the swallow-tailed design, although it may have been copied from European lance pennons. Colors: dark blue canton with gold stars, seven red and six white stripes.

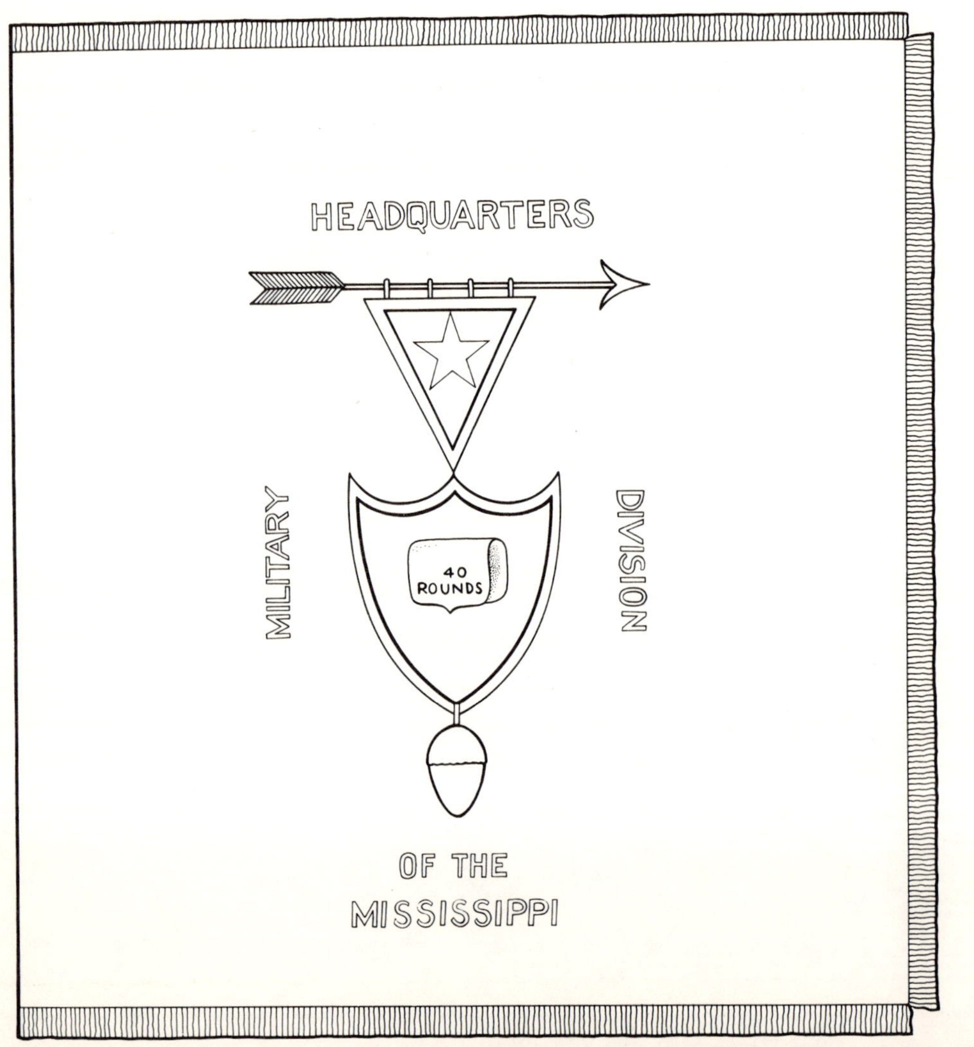

MILITARY DIVISION
OF THE MISSISSIPPI
HEADQUARTERS FLAG

Special badges were adopted by various corps for identification on uniforms and elsewhere. Arrows, stars, crosses, eagles, crescents, acorns and other designs were favored. Several of these can be seen combined in the flag which identified the headquarters of the Military Division of the Mississippi under General William Tecumseh Sherman. The flag may have been used as early as the Chattanooga Campaign. If so, it must have been plain yellow because some of the corps badges were not adopted until very late in the war. Colors: yellow background; crimson inscription and emblems, except for yellow star and cartridge box; light blue fringe.

The different divisions of the 15th Army Corps had flags of a solid color—red for the 1st, white for the 2nd, blue for the 3rd, and yellow for the 4th. Each had in the center a representation of a cartridge box with a medallion bearing the letters US and the words FORTY ROUNDS. The headquarters flag combined the four colors of the division. The cartridge box, if indeed it carried 40 rounds, must have been extremely heavy. The normal cartridge box had 20, and soldiers often split these up to balance the weight on either side of their belts. Colors: the four quarters (clockwise from the upper left-hand corner) are red, white, dark blue and dark yellow. The inscriptions are black; the cartridge box is light brown with a gold oval.

Florida seceded from the Union on 11 January 1861. Two days later the commander of its armed forces prescribed a temporary flag that looked like the Stars and Stripes but had only a single star in the canton. In September 1861 the governor established a permanent flag. The seal shows an oak growing near the Gulf of Mexico with a ship and weapons. Colors: horizontal stripes are red, white, red; vertical stripe is blue; inscription is blue on a white band; the seal design is colored from nature.

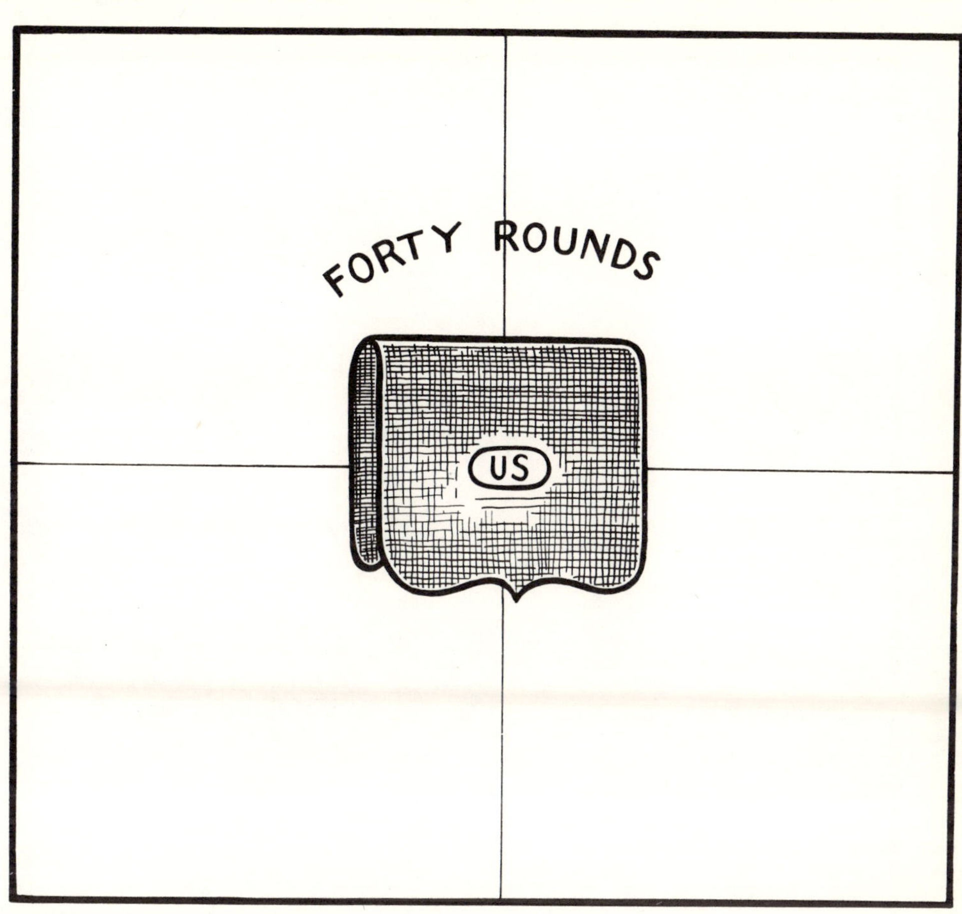

15th ARMY CORPS HEADQUARTERS FLAG

FLORIDA FLAG

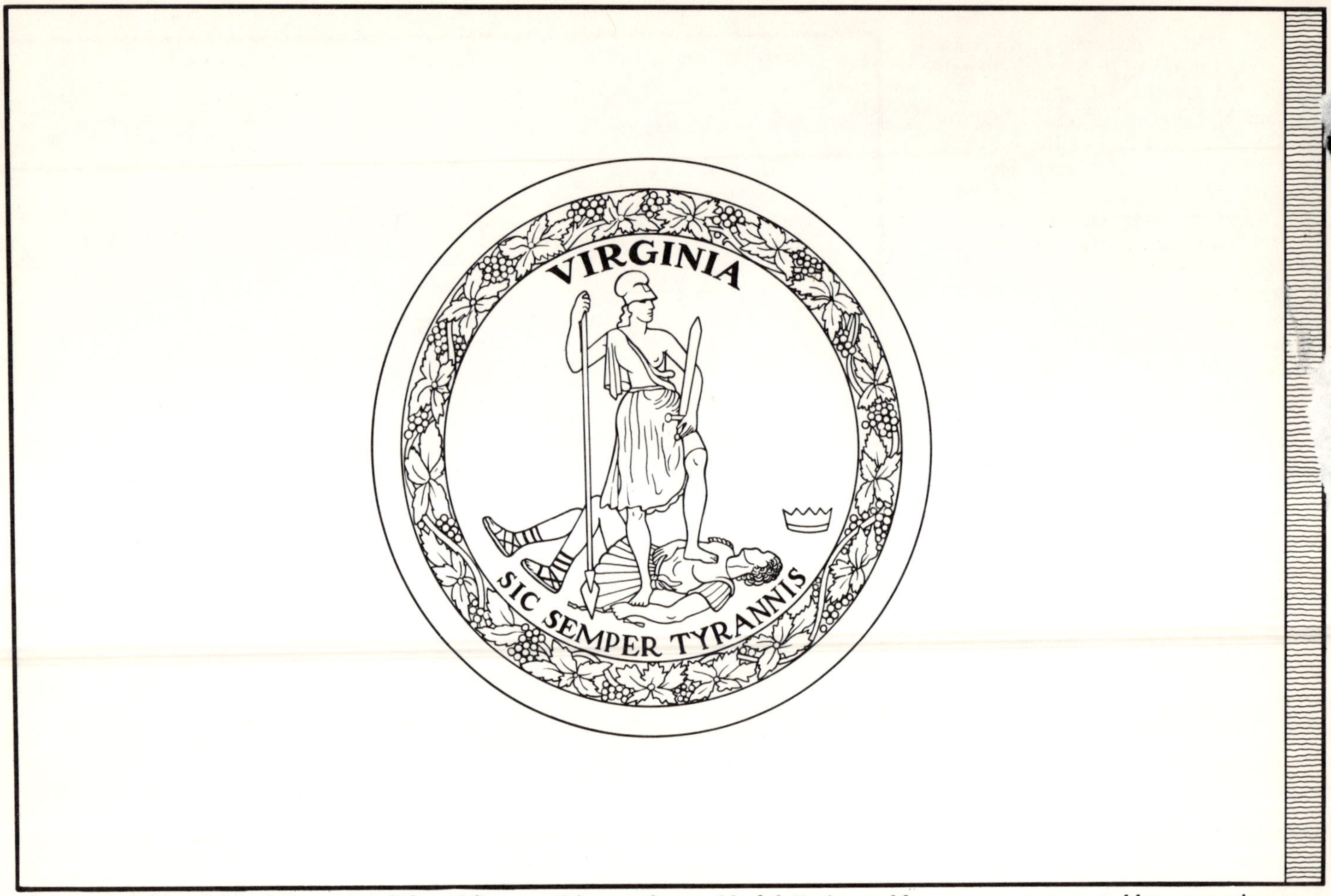

Colors: dark blue field; white central disk; red flowers with green leaves; black lettering; gold crown; woman wears blue, man crimson; the other parts of the design are in natural colors.

VIRGINIA FLAG

In 1861 Virginia adopted a flag at the time of its secession from the Union. The state seal appearing on that flag, however, dates back to the American Revolution. The central figure is a woman in Amazon dress representing Virginia and holding a spear and sword. She stands on a man representing tyranny who holds a whip and chain. His crown lies to one side. The motto makes clear the significance—"Thus Ever to Tyrants." That was the phrase shouted by John Wilkes Booth, leaping to the stage of the theater after he had assassinated Lincoln.

In May 1864 the Stars and Stripes were replaced by this flag for use at the headquarters of the Army of the Potomac. The central design is clearly of Roman inspiration. General Grant is supposed to have been shocked when he saw it. He exclaimed, "What's this! Is Imperial Caesar anywhere about here?"

ARMY
OF THE POTOMAC
HEADQUARTERS FLAG

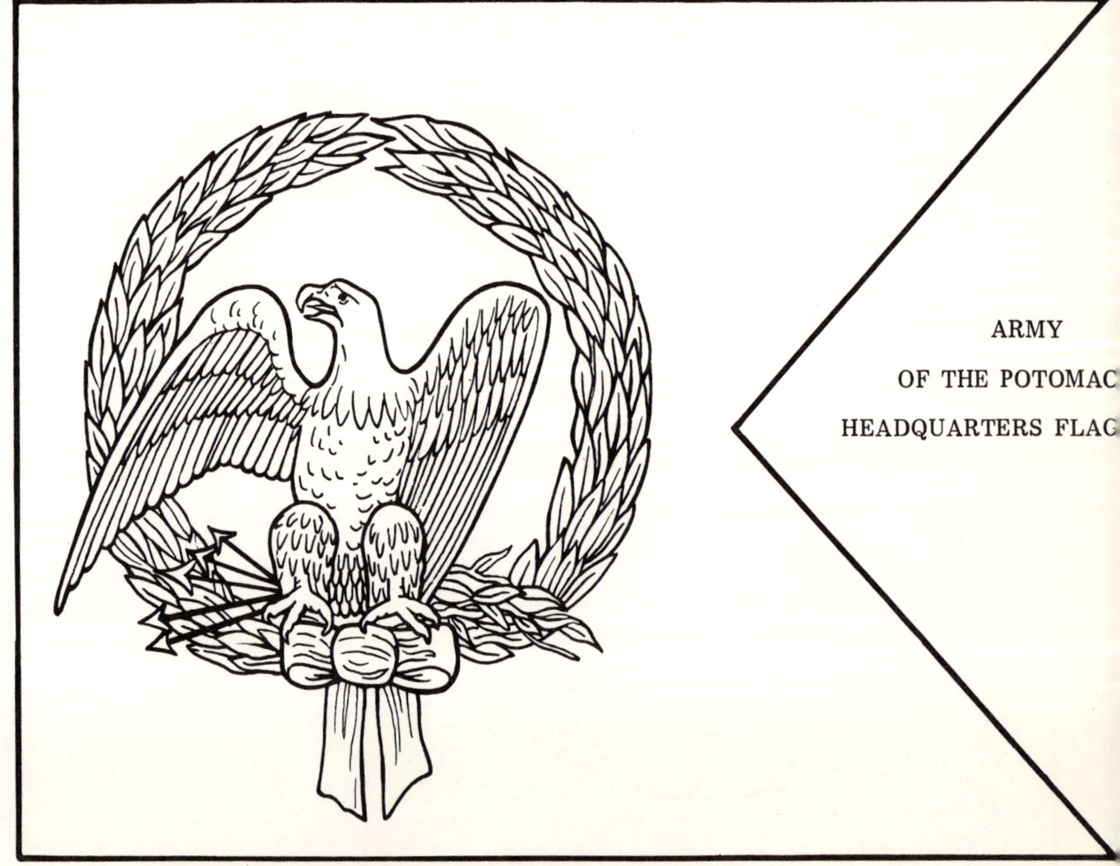

Colors: light reddish purple background; gold eagle, arrows, and laurel; silver wreath and ribbon.